KNOW YOUR RIGHTS™

YOUR LEGAL RIGHTS AS A JUVENILE TRIED AS AN ADULT

CRISTEN NAGLE

ROSEN PUBLISHING
New York

Published in 2015 by The Rosen Publishing Group, Inc.
29 East 21st Street, New York, NY 10010

First Edition

Expert Reviewer: Lindsay A. Lewis, Esq.

Library of Congress Cataloging-in-Publication Data

Nagle, Cristen, author.
Your legal rights as a juvenile being tried as an adult/Cristen Nagle.—
First Edition.
pages cm.—(Know your rights)
Includes bibliographical references and index.
ISBN 978-1-4777-8016-9 (library bound)—ISBN 978-1-4777-8017-6
(pbk.)—ISBN 978-1-4777-8018-3 (6-pack)
1. Juvenile justice, Administration of—United States—Juvenile
literature. 2. Juvenile courts—United States—Juvenile literature.
I. Title.
KF9779.N34 2015
345.73'08—dc23

2014021709

Manufactured in the United States of America

CONTENTS

INTRODUCTION

Every American has rights. One of the most important is liberty. This is the right to walk, live, and breathe wherever you want. The Constitution gives Americans certain rights to keep the government from taking away or limiting their liberty. These are called constitutional rights.

However, the American justice system does place some limits on citizens' liberties. The justice system is made up of police, courts, and prisons. It catches and punishes people who break the law. People's constitutional rights protect them against abuses within this system and guarantee their fair treatment under the law. Constitutional rights are the best protection from the justice system, so people need to know what those rights are. They have to know what their rights mean and understand the system in order to use them at the right time.

Consider the following scenario: John is walking down the street when he sees a laptop sitting in an open window. Nobody is around, so he reaches through the window and picks it up. He slips it into his backpack and continues down the street. The laptop's owner, Anthony, reports the theft to a police officer. As the officer is leaving Anthony's home, she passes John in a park. On a hunch, she picks up the backpack sitting a few feet away from him. She unzips the backpack, looks inside, and sees the laptop. John is arrested and confesses to taking the laptop.

When his case goes to trial, he is convicted of larceny and sentenced to thirty days in prison.

What John didn't realize is that the officer violated his constitutional rights by searching his bag on no more than a hunch. The officer's search was not allowed by the

The government can take away liberty from those who don't follow the rules. While there are some rights the government can never take away, the accused has to "use or lose" many of these rights. That's why knowing your rights is the best defense.

Constitution. The government could not use the fact that the officer found the laptop in John's backpack to prove that he was guilty of larceny. If John had not confessed, he could have walked away a free man. However, he did not know his rights.

It is especially important for minors—those under eighteen years old—to know their rights because they can be tried as adults in some cases. The United States has one justice system that was set up to deal with adults and another that was set up to deal with minors. The adult system is called the criminal justice system. The system for minors is the juvenile-justice system. It was set up to take into account the facts that minors are not fully developed and their behavior tends to be more malleable, or easily influenced. The juvenile justice system is designed not just to punish, but also to guide and support minors who have broken the law. However, minors can be tried in either system. This means that they need to understand how both systems work. For example, the penalties in the criminal-justice system are generally more severe than those in the juvenile-justice system. The difference between the two systems can be the difference between being free to live a normal, productive life and being saddled with an adult conviction on your permanent record.

This book will help minors understand the criminal- and juvenile-justice systems, as well as the differences between them. It can help minors who are, or may someday find themselves, in trouble with the law understand who decides how they will be treated and how that decision is made. Minors armed with this knowledge are better prepared to exercise their rights and keep their liberty.

CHAPTER 1

WHERE DOES THE LAW COME FROM?

The United States Constitution is the document that created the American government and gives all the people in the government their power. The Constitution allows the government to pass laws, which are rules that everyone must follow. Laws say what people can and can't do and set a punishment for people who break them. Laws are not allowed to be unconstitutional, or contradict the Constitution. The Constitution has twenty-seven amendments, or additions that have been added over the years. The Bill of Rights is the first ten amendments, or additions, to the Constitution. It gives Americans key rights that the government can never take away. Every state also has its own state constitution. At the very least, a state must grant its residents the same rights guaranteed under the U.S. Constitution. However, many states provide for extra rights and protections that go beyond those in the U.S. Constitution.

The U.S. Constitution creates the three branches of the federal government: the executive branch, the legislative branch, and the judicial branch. The executive branch is responsible for enforcing the laws of the land. The legislative branch passes laws. The judicial branch is responsible for figuring out what the laws mean and whether they are constitutional. Courts can't make laws. However, they can

Many people find themselves in situations in which their rights conflict with another's. Judges are the only people who can resolve cases of competing rights. The Supreme Court, seen here, often needs to consider competing rights in the cases it sees.

decide whether the government has acted improperly under the law or misinterpreted a law. The Supreme Court can also declare laws unconstitutional. The Constitution says that all three branches of government must be equal, so no branch is more powerful than the others.

THE COURT SYSTEM

The court system is made up of three court levels. The first level is a trial court, where innocence or guilt is

THE LAYERS OF GOVERNMENT

Government in the United States has three layers. They are the governments, federal governments, state governments, and local governments. The highest is the federal government, which includes the president, Congress, and the U.S. Supreme Court. Under the Supreme Court in the judicial branch are circuit courts of appeal and district courts. Every federal court has power over the whole federal government. A district court can undo something the president does if it is unconstitutional.

Each of the fifty states has its own court system. State court systems usually have three levels, just like the federal court system, with even the lowest state court having power over the whole state government. Local courts, such as municipal courts, city courts, and county courts, are part of the state court system.

In general, the punishments if a defendant is convicted are harsher in a federal court. State courts tend to have less harsh punishments, while those coming out of local courts are the least harsh. Sometimes a defendant will be charged in both state and federal court, because he or she has broken both state and federal laws. In that case, the federal trial will come first.

decided. The middle level is an appeals court, which looks at what happened at the trial court and decides whether there were any mistakes. The third level is a higher appeals court, which looks at what both lower courts did. Federal trial courts are called district courts. Midlevel federal courts are called circuit courts of appeal, and the highest-level federal court is the United States Supreme Court.

The U.S. court system can be very confusing because federal and state courts each have their own names and special rules. Defendants who are charged with violating federal laws are tried in federal courts, while defendants charged with violating state laws are tried in state courts. State trial and appeal courts are called different things depending on the state. Both the state courts and the federal courts must follow Supreme Court precedent and both state and federal defendants can appeal their cases to the Supreme Court as a court of last resort.

Federal courts get their power from the Constitution. Who and what they have power over is called jurisdiction. Only federal courts have jurisdiction over federal laws. This means that state courts don't have the power to decide whether a federal law is fair or if someone has broken it. State courts get their power from their state's constitutions and have jurisdiction over (1) state laws, (2) property located inside the state, and (3) people who live or are passing through the state.

Take, for example, the imaginary case of Anthony, who lives in New Jersey. Anthony visits John in New York. They get in a fight and John grabs Anthony's cell phone. This is not illegal in New York, but it is against the law in New Jersey. Anthony goes back to New Jersey and tries to have John arrested. New Jersey has no jurisdiction over John because John neither lives nor owns property in New Jersey, and he did not break a New Jersey law while in New Jersey.

Every case starts with a police officer because, just as it says, law enforcement is charged with enforcing the law. Every officer is part of the government, so your constitutional rights kick in the moment an officer speaks to you.

MOVING THROUGH THE COURTS

Before a case can move on to a higher court, it must be tried in a trial court. Trials may be before a jury or a judge without a jury. A trial with a judge and no jury is called a bench trial. Unless a person pleads guilty, only a jury or a trial court judge can decide whether that person is guilty or innocent of a crime.

Trial courts have civil and criminal parts. Many states also have special parts for different kinds of cases.

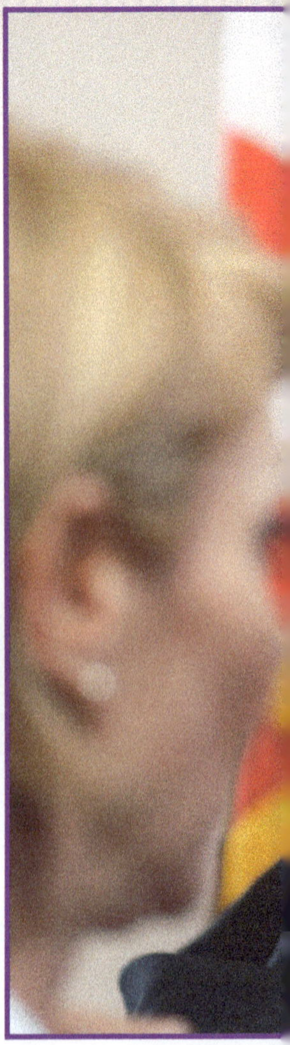

Domestic-violence courts, small-claims courts, drug courts, and family courts are examples of special trial courts. Juvenile courts are special trial courts specially designed for minors. Juvenile and criminal courts often have concurrent jurisdiction over minors. This means both have power over their cases. Where a minor's case will go and who decides will depend on the state.

Whoever loses at the trial level can ask the next-level court to look at what the trial court did and decide whether any mistakes were made. The mid-level court is called appeals court or appellate court. A request for a higher court to reconsider the ruling of a lower court is called an appeal. In most states, the defendant has one appeal "as of right" to the intermediate-level court (the lower court of appeals) unless the right to appeal has been waived. An appeal "as of right" is a guaranteed appeal. The appeals court has to agree to hear the case. However, appeals to the highest state or federal appellate courts are discretionary. This means that it is up to the appellate courts to decide whether to hear these cases. It is important to file a notice of appeal in time in order to preserve the right to appeal your case. Appeals courts don't decide whether a jury's verdict or a judge's decision is right or wrong. They decide only whether there were any legal issues with the earlier trial.

While most cases stay in either the state court system or the federal court system, there is one exception. If the highest state appellate court refuses to hear your case or denies your appeal, you might be able to appeal your

Trial court judges have the most discretion, or flexibility, because they see and hear witnesses and are in the best position to judge credibility. Trial judges decide what evidence can be admitted at trial, which can have a big impact on the outcome of a case.

case to the U.S. Supreme Court. However, this can happen only if it can be argued that there was a violation of the U.S. Constitution in your case. This is a discretionary appeal, so it is up to the Supreme Court to decide whether to hear the case. No case can go higher than the Supreme Court.

CHAPTER 2

WHAT IS THE LAW?

Laws are meant to prohibit crimes, which can be broken down into three general categories. Crimes against people are those in which force is threatened or used against another person. Murder and assault are examples of crimes against people because people are the victims. Crimes against property have someone's possessions as the victim. Examples include arson and vandalism. Crimes against the public have a lot of people as victims. For example, corruption by politicians or other government officials is a

Minors accused of serious or violent crimes are more likely to be tried as adults. Understanding the law can help minors avoid the behaviors that can land them in adult prison for the rest of their lives.

crime against the public because everybody who pays taxes is a victim.

CRIMINAL LAW

There are two kinds of laws, criminal and civil. The difference between the two has to do with the punishments attached to breaking them. Violating a civil law results in money being taken away from the one who is convicted, while a conviction for violating criminal laws typically results in the loss of a person's liberty.

Criminal laws can be boiled down into two general rules: (1) don't use or threaten force against another person or their property and (2) don't help someone else break the law.

Regarding the first rule, someone who hurts or threatens to hurt another will be guilty of a crime unless they had a good enough reason, or legal justification. The most common legal justification is self-defense: people whose lives are being threatened with force are allowed to use force against the people threatening them. Thus, someone being kidnapped would not be prosecuted for biting his or her attacker even though it is against the law (it is considered assault) because the attacker is threatening the person's life. In other words, the person had legal justification to use force in resisting and is not guilty of a crime.

Regarding the second rule, it does not matter how little or how much someone helps another commit a crime. It is a crime to help at all. However, how much a person helps will make a difference in the punishment he or she receives. A getaway driver who planned and took part in robbing a bank will be punished more than someone who was driving by, saw his friend running, and gave him a ride, not knowing he had robbed a bank. The getaway driver will be punished for the whole robbery even though he waited outside, while the person who gave his friend a ride can only be punished for being an accessory after the fact. One may be sent to jail for years, while the other might not even be charged.

Of course, there are more rules than just these two. For example, it is illegal to help someone avoid getting arrested or to be part of a conspiracy. People can't go on, take, or damage someone else's private property or refuse to leave the property when asked. They can't make, sell, or use drugs, lie under oath, or ignore a court order.

CONSTITUTIONAL RIGHTS

It is not illegal to be part of a group that is not breaking the law. The First Amendment gives Americans the right to free speech and the right to assemble, or gather together. The right to free speech means that, with a few exceptions, people can talk to whomever they want about whatever they want. The exceptions include

All minors accused of crimes have the right to remain silent; they do not have to talk to the police. Minors have the right to an attorney and should ask for a lawyer as soon as they are placed under arrest.

things such as obscenity and speech that is meant to stir up violence.

The Fifth Amendment gives Americans the right not to incriminate themselves. Incriminate means "to say or do something that makes you look guilty of a crime." The right against self-incrimination is also called the right to remain silent. Americans have the right not to talk to the police, and it is not against the law to invoke, or use, this right. A person can always invoke his right to remain silent, even when he is are testifying in another case.

As an example, let's say John and Anthony steal someone's purse but only John gets caught. John is on trial and Anthony is called as a witness. The prosecutor asks Anthony whether he was with John when John stole the purse. Anthony does not have to answer because if he says "yes," then he could be arrested and charged with stealing the purse.

The Fifth Amendment also gives Americans the right not to be tried twice for the same crime. This is called double jeopardy. Double jeopardy doesn't mean that a person can't be arrested more than once for the same crime. Suspects can be arrested, released, and rearrested without violating the Constitution. However, no one can be put on trial twice for the same crime. Double jeopardy does not mean that someone found guilty of robbery can never be tried for robbery again. They can be tried for robbery as many times as they commit robbery. They just can't be tried more than once for a particular robbery.

As an example of this scenario, John robs Anthony on Christmas Eve. John is arrested and put on trial. Anthony is the only witness, but the jury doesn't believe him and finds John not guilty. John robs Anthony again the next day. While investigating, the police find someone who saw John robbing Anthony on Christmas Eve. John can't be tried again for robbing Anthony on Christmas Eve, even though there is a new witness, because he already has been tried for that crime. However, John can be tried for robbing Anthony the second time.

DUE PROCESS

The Fifth Amendment to the United States Constitution says that the federal government can't take away an American's life, liberty, or property without "due process of law." The Fourteenth Amendment says the individual states can't do so either. Due process means that people must receive notice that the government is going to take something away and must be given a chance to fight it. Because criminal laws take the most liberty, those accused of breaking them have the right to the most due process. They have the right to a fair trial, part of which is the right to be presumed innocent. The presumption of innocence means that it is assumed that defendants are innocent unless and until they are proven guilty. The government can't put people in jail as punishment until there has been a fair trial because that would be treating them as if they were guilty. They can be put in jail for other reasons, such as to protect the public or to make sure they show up for the trial. But they can't be punished for a crime until their guilt has been proven.

The government has to prove a criminal defendant's guilt "beyond a reasonable doubt." A reasonable doubt is a doubt based in reason and arising out of the

While adult criminal defendants have the right to a jury trial, juvenile-court defendants do not. However, both must have their guilt proven beyond a reasonable doubt.

evidence in the case, or the lack of evidence. It is a doubt that a reasonable person has after carefully weighing all of the evidence in the case.

BEARING THE BURDEN OF PROOF

Proving that something is true beyond a reasonable doubt is what is called the burden of proof. This concept concerns how convincing the evidence against someone has to be. Beyond a reasonable doubt is the highest burden of proof because the most liberty is at stake. Other burdens of proof include "preponderance of the evidence," meaning enough of the evidence proves that something is more likely than not to be true, and "clear and convincing evidence," in which the evidence is convincing even though there could be other explanations.

The government has to show that someone is guilty of each "element," or part, of the crime. In all cases, the government must prove that a person both meant to and actually did commit a criminal act. To convict someone of a particular crime, the government must prove that that person is guilty of all the elements of that crime. The elements of each crime are spelled out in the law itself. For example, in New York State, a person is guilty of first-degree robbery if the government can prove beyond a reasonable doubt that he (1) forcibly stole property and (2) while stealing that property or

JANE AND THE ALIEN ABDUCTION

John, Anthony, and Jane are hanging out in a park. Jane says she has to go to the bathroom and walks into some nearby woods. After about ten minutes, John and Anthony wonder where Jane went. John goes looking for Jane while Anthony waits in the park. John comes back about five minutes later and says he can't find Jane. Jane is never seen or heard from again.

John is arrested and charged with Jane's murder. At trial, John testifies that he did not kill Jane and either someone else did or she was abducted by aliens. The only other witness at trial is Anthony, who testifies that he killed Jane while John was in the woods. If the jury believes Anthony, his confession is evidence that someone else committed the crime. Doubting that John did it would be reasonable, and the jury would have to find John not guilty.

It would not be reasonable for the jury to doubt John did it because aliens might have abducted Jane. There is no evidence of that and common sense tells us that probably didn't happen. The jury would have to find John guilty because the government would have proven his guilt beyond a *reasonable* doubt.

fleeing from stealing that property, (3) he or another participant in the crime either (a) caused serious physical injury to someone who was not a participant in the crime, (b) was armed with a deadly weapon, (c) used or threatened the use of a dangerous instrument, or (d) displayed a firearm.

Some crimes, including robbery, have different degrees. The different degrees are measures of how serious a crime is. For example, a person is guilty of robbery in the third degree when he forcibly steals property. That charge goes up to second-degree robbery if (1) he is helped by another person at the scene of the crime, (2) during or while fleeing from the crime, he either (a) injures a person who was not a participant in the crime, or (b) shows what looks like a firearm, or (3) the property being stolen is a car. The more serious a charge is, the more severe the punishment for it is.

ASSURED REPRESENTATION

The Sixth Amendment gives everyone accused of breaking a criminal law the right to a lawyer. This is part of making sure that everyone gets a fair trial. If someone can't afford a lawyer, the government must pay for one. The right to a lawyer does not mean the right to the best lawyer or a perfect lawyer. It just means the right to a lawyer who will meet with you, come up with a plan for defending you, and try to get the best result for you. A lawyer can help a defendant use her Sixth Amendment rights to know what she is accused of and to confront the witnesses against her. The lawyer will know which questions to ask at a trial to find out if a witness is lying or whether her client's constitutional rights are being violated in court. Before the trial, a lawyer can file legal papers called motions. These may challenge the charges against her client. They may also uncover whether the police violated any of her client's rights.

Even though juvenile courts are civil, minors' liberty is still at risk because they can be sent to

A lawyer is a minor's strongest ally in the court system. Lawyers know and understand the law and the system. Everything their clients tell them is confidential.

juvenile-detention centers or other places where their movements will be restricted. Juveniles therefore have many of the same rights as criminal defendants. They have the right to remain silent and the right to a lawyer. They have to right to confront their accusers and the right to be presumed innocent. Juveniles are protected by double jeopardy, and their guilt must be proven "beyond a reasonable doubt."

CHAPTER 3

WHAT IS JUVENILE COURT AND WHY IS IT DIFFERENT?

Juvenile courts are special courts for minors who are accused of doing something that would be a crime if an adult did it. Minors are defined as people younger than eighteen who are dependent upon their parents for basic life needs, such as food and housing. While one of the goals of the juvenile-justice system is to discipline minors who commit crimes, it also aims to help minors avoid criminal behavior by providing education, treatment, and discipline. It helps minors deal with personal, social, and family issues in a healthy way, in hopes that they will grow into responsible adults. Juvenile courts step in for parents who need help giving their children guidance and support.

THE DIFFERENCES BETWEEN MINORS AND ADULTS

Separate systems for minors and adults are necessary because minors and adults are very different. Adults have more education and experience. They can understand and control what is going on around them. Adult brains are fully developed, which means that adults can control their emotions and their reactions.

Minors, on the other hand, are still developing. Their brains are still growing, and they do not have the same ability to control their emotions and behavior that adults do. Minors are more likely to follow along with a group. They are less likely to understand the consequences of their actions. Most minors tend to focus only on the good

Understanding that kids might not yet "know better" because they are still growing, lawmakers created juvenile courts to avoid punishing kids for doing things they haven't yet learned are wrong.

things that might happen if they do something, like having fun and feeling good. They don't think about the bad things that could happen, like hurting someone or getting arrested. Minors are less likely to understand that what they are doing is wrong, especially if they are learning the behavior from adults. They know less about the law and the justice system, making them easier to manipulate. Minors can't drink alcohol, vote, or do a lot of other things that adults

AN EXAMPLE OF CULPABILITY

John is forty and his son Anthony is eight. They are out looking for food because John lost his job and the family hasn't eaten in four days. They are walking past a convenience store when John calls Anthony over. He tells Anthony that they are going to get some food from this store. He will talk to the store clerk while Anthony puts a loaf of bread under his coat. Anthony asks if that is stealing. John says yes, but it's okay to do if your family is starving. Anthony follows his dad into the store and puts the bread in his coat while John talks to the clerk. Then they both walk out.

If they are arrested and charged with theft, John will be punished but Anthony will not. Anthony was doing what his dad asked him to do. He can't get a job at the convenience store to earn money to buy food, and he can't take out a loan to buy the bread. Anthony can't just walk away because he is eight and is still under his dad's control. John, on the other hand, knew that stealing was wrong. He could do odd jobs to get money or could apply for food stamps instead of stealing bread. Therefore, John would be culpable while Anthony would not be.

can. Since they can't control their life circumstances, minors have a harder time getting away from criminal situations. All of these factors mean that minors are not as culpable, or blameworthy, as adults.

PAYING THE PRICE OR DOING THE TIME

A juvenile case starts with an arrest. From there, the case might keep going to juvenile court or the juvenile might be allowed to do community service. The juvenile might also pay money to make up for whatever he or she did. This is called restitution. A case won't be sent to juvenile court once the juvenile completes the community service or makes restitution. If the case is sent to juvenile court, the prosecutor will file a petition. This is a piece of paper accusing a minor of doing something that would be a crime if an adult did it. In criminal court this piece of paper would be called an indictment. The petition has to say exactly what the minor did, when the offense was committed, and what precise law has been broken. Once a juvenile case has started, it might go all the way through the juvenile court or the prosecutor and juvenile might make a deal.

If the case goes to trial, the juvenile-court judge will hear evidence about what the minor is accused of doing.

Many juveniles can avoid harsher punishments by doing community service. This can be a great way for juveniles to make new friends or learn new skills.

The judge will decide whether the juvenile is "delinquent," or guilty of doing things that would be a crime if an adult did them. Delinquency has to be proven "beyond a reasonable doubt." Then the juvenile-court judge will try to figure out what kind of services each juvenile needs and whether

MOVING TARGETS

The job of a juvenile-court judge is to know every juvenile's problem and how to fix it. This is really hard because every juvenile is different. Many minors in the juvenile system have difficult home lives or have gone through traumatic events. They may not want to talk about this to strangers. They might not trust adults or "the system." When a juvenile can't or won't talk to a judge, it's hard for that judge to understand the juvenile's behavior and what services would help him or her. Even if a juvenile participates, the judge is faced with a moving target because juveniles change over time. Their personalities, their friends, and their family situations will be different every time the judge sees them. Yet a juvenile-court judge is supposed to know what services will help a juvenile in the future and which juveniles are likely to continue to break the rules.

getting those services will put him on the right track. Juvenile-court judges also have to protect the public from violent juveniles. Judges can order therapy, job training, drug treatment, family counseling, education, and countless other services for the juvenile. They can send minors who they think are dangerous to live in detention centers or group homes. This is also where they send juveniles who have no safe place to live.

Juveniles can be held before and after their trials. Because pretrial juvenile detention can seem like punishment, minors have a due process right to a hearing before or very soon after they are held. However, they do not have a right to bail. Bail is money criminal defendants can pay

Many juveniles who become involved in the system need, but are not getting, social services. Juvenile courts offer counseling, education, career training, and many other support programs that minors might not otherwise have access to.

the court in exchange for freedom before their trial. The bail money is meant to ensure the person shows up for trial. Those who come to court will get their bail money back. The court will keep the money of those who don't. Juveniles don't have a right to bail because their proceedings are civil. In some cases, the system assumes that juveniles have been charged with delinquency because they are not being watched at home, making it necessary to house them somewhere else.

CHAPTER 4

JUVENILE OR CRIMINAL COURT: WHO DECIDES AND HOW?

No one eighteen or over can be tried as a juvenile, but someone under eighteen can be tried as an adult. How that person will be treated will depend on what she did and where she lives. Every state and the federal government allow juvenile cases to be "transferred," or moved, to adult criminal court. There are three types of transfer laws. Statutory exclusion laws automatically exclude certain juveniles from juvenile court. *Statute* is another word for "law." Direct file laws let prosecutors decide whether to try a minor as a juvenile or as an adult. Waiver laws let judges decide. Most states and the federal government have a mix of each kind of law. This makes it hard to know who will decide where a minor will be tried and how that decision will be made.

STATUTORY EXCLUSION LAWS

Statutory exclusion laws are the easiest to understand. Age-based exclusion laws ban people over a certain age from juvenile court. For the federal government and most

The quickest way for a minor to know if she will be treated as an adult is to know the maximum age for juvenile court in her state. A minor can check her local court's website to find out this information.

states that age is eighteen. Two states exclude juveniles over fifteen, and eleven states exclude juveniles over sixteen. Minors who are too old for juvenile court in their state will automatically go to criminal court.

Offense-based laws exclude those accused of committing certain crimes from juvenile court. These are usually serious and violent crimes against people or property. Drug and weapons offenses are also frequently excluded from juvenile court. The idea behind these laws is that juveniles should do "adult time for adult crime." Some states and the federal government exclude "repeat offenders" from juvenile court. These are minors

TWO SCENARIOS

These two scenarios demonstrate the importance of knowing the age of exclusion from juvenile court. In the first scenario, John is sixteen and lives in New York. New York's juvenile court excludes people older than fifteen. If John assaults Anthony, he will automatically go to criminal court and be treated and punished like an adult.

In the second scenario, John gets caught taking two ounces of marijuana from New York to New Jersey. That is a federal crime, so John can be tried in federal court either as an adult or as a juvenile. It does not matter that John is considered an adult under New York state law.

Native American juveniles are subject to federal law while they are on a reservation and to state law when they are off.

who have committed crimes before. This means that the cases of minors with any kind of record will go to criminal court no matter how petty their newest offenses are. Federal courts exclude repeat offenders over the age of sixteen who are accused of certain violent crimes from juvenile court.

Native American juveniles who live on reservations will be tried as adults in federal court if they are accused of committing a "major crime," while less serious offenses will be tried in tribal courts. A Native American juvenile who lives on a reservation and commits a crime while off the reservation will be tried in state instead of federal court. Native American minors who do not live on reservations will be sent to state court no matter what crime they are accused of committing. Whether these Native American juveniles are tried as adults or juveniles will depend on the laws of the state they live in.

DIRECT FILE LAWS

In direct file states, the prosecutor will decide whether to send a case to juvenile or criminal court. It is a prosecutor's job to get justice for victims and protect society. When deciding how to prosecute a minor, a prosecutor is also supposed to look at the minor's age, what he or she is accused of doing, and the circumstances. The prosecutor will look at the minor's record to see if he or she has been in trouble before and for what. However, the minor's personal circumstances are third in line of importance behind justice for the victim and public safety. The seriousness of the crime and any threat to the public will be more important to the prosecutor than the minor's situation. The prosecutor does not have to meet with the minor's attorney, probation officer, teachers, or anyone else before deciding to try the minor as an adult. There is no hearing, and the prosecutor doesn't need a judge's permission. The prosecutor's decision will be final, which means an appeals court can't look at it and decide whether it's wrong. The

Although prosecutors work at the courthouse, they do not work for the courts. Courts and judges are impartial, while prosecutors are the lawyers for, and on the side of, the state.

minor will know whether he or she will be tried as a juvenile or as an adult when the prosecutor files either a petition or an indictment.

A QUICK GUIDE: JUVENILE OR ADULT?

1. Is the person under eighteen?
   If no, the person will go to criminal court. If yes...
2. Is the person too old for juvenile court in the state?
   If yes, the person will go to criminal court. If no...
3. Is the person accused of a serious crime, such as murder, arson, robbery, or a weapons or drug offense?
   If yes, the person will go to criminal court. If no...
4. Has the prosecutor asked a judge to transfer the person's case?
   If no, the person will go to juvenile court. If yes...
5. Has the judge ruled that the case should be transferred?
   If yes, the person will go to criminal court. If no, the person will go to juvenile court.

WAIVER LAWS

Waiver laws give judges the power to decide where a juvenile will be tried. To waive means "to give up," and waiver laws let judges give up their court's power over a juvenile. This is called waiving jurisdiction. There are two types of waiver laws. Judicial waiver laws give juvenile-court judges the power to waive jurisdiction. Reverse waiver laws give that power to criminal-court judges. Judicial waivers involve a juvenile-court prosecutor asking a judge to transfer a juvenile case to criminal court. Reverse waivers involve a juvenile who is being tried as an adult asking a criminal-court judge to send the case to juvenile court. For a waiver to be granted, the juvenile must meet all of the other requirements for juvenile court. He or she must be young enough and not accused of a crime that is excluded. Juveniles who live in direct file states should find out whether their state also allows reverse waivers. It may be the only way to undo a prosecutor's choice of criminal court.

No matter where a case is started, minors have a due process right to a hearing before their cases can be transferred. They have the right to a lawyer at this hearing. Minors can offer any evidence they want to show that their behavior would improve with treatment, making juvenile court the right place for them. Judges deciding whether to transfer cases have to provide a written decision stating their exact reasons for waiving or not waiving jurisdiction.

Many waiver laws are accompanied by a presumption that juveniles over a certain age or accused of certain crimes will not get better with treatment. The presumption is that these juveniles should be treated as adults. The presumption can be overcome with evidence that the minor is unlikely to commit more crimes if he gets help. If a judge is convinced by this evidence, that judge can keep the case in juvenile court. If the judge does not believe the evidence or if there is no evidence, the presumption applies and the case will go to criminal court.

Crimes against people and those involving drugs or weapons are more likely to be transferred to criminal court. The more violent or serious the crime, the more likely a juvenile will be tried as an adult. Each subsequent offense also increases a minor's chances of being

Minors accused of drug crimes are more likely to be tried as adults, as are repeat offenders and those accused of weapons offenses and violent crimes.

treated like an adult. Some states even have "once an adult, always an adult" laws saying that minors who have been treated as adults in the past will always be treated that way in the future. It won't matter what the juvenile is accused of or if a case would normally go to juvenile court. Being treated as an adult once means the minor can never go to juvenile court again.

CHAPTER 5

JUVENILE OR ADULT: WHY DOES IT MATTER?

Whether a minor is treated as a juvenile or an adult matters. Which system a minor is in determines how he or she will be tried and sentenced. There are some protections for people on trial that exist in the criminal court system, but not in the juvenile one. On the other hand, minors who are tried in criminal courts tend to receive harsher sentences than those charged in juvenile courts. A criminal conviction is more likely to make a minor's life difficult in the long run, too.

DIFFERENCES AT THE TRIAL

Unlike adult criminal defendants, juveniles do not have the right to a public trial. The media and other members of the public are not allowed to watch juvenile proceedings. While this means that a juvenile's mistakes stay a secret, it could also change how a judge rules because no one is watching. Also, a juvenile trial might take longer than a criminal trial because juveniles don't have the same right to a speedy trial.

Criminal courts, which try adults, have special rules of evidence to make sure that no evidence is used against a person in violation of his or her rights. Juvenile-court judges have fewer rules to follow. For example, juvenile

Whether tried as an adult or as a juvenile, a person found not guilty of a crime will not have a criminal record.

court judges can consider hearsay testimony while criminal-court judges generally cannot. Hearsay comes in many forms. The most basic form is something someone other than the person testifying said being used as evidence that whatever that first person said was true.

For example, let's say that Jane is on trial in criminal court for robbery. Anthony tells John that Jane admitted to him that she had committed the robbery. If John testifies at Jane's trial about what Anthony said, his testimony would be hearsay. After all, he is just repeating what Anthony told him Jane said. If Jane's trial were in a criminal court, John's testimony would be inadmissible. This means it would not be allowed at Jane's trial. This is because Jane has the right to face her accuser, who is Anthony. On the other hand, John's testimony would probably be allowed in juvenile court.

JUVENILE DELINQUENTS AND JUVENILE OFFENDERS

A juvenile who has been tried and convicted in criminal court is called a juvenile offender, while a juvenile found guilty of doing things that would be a crime if an adult did them is called a juvenile delinquent. Juveniles do not have the right to a jury trial and instead are tried before a juvenile-court judge. This matters because, statistically, juries are more likely to find someone not guilty than are judges. The fates of juveniles rest entirely in the hands of the juvenile court judge, so not having a jury could mean that a juvenile is more likely to be found delinquent than not guilty.

The biggest difference between juvenile offenders and juvenile delinquents is how they are sentenced. Juvenile-court judges have the power to do whatever they want in sentencing, which is called discretion. Juvenile-court judges have a lot of discretion because it is their job to make a unique sentence for each juvenile. There can't be one rule for everyone because every juvenile is different. Before sentencing a delinquent juvenile, a judge will talk to the juvenile and the juvenile's family. He will meet with the juvenile-probation department, teachers, therapists, and anyone else who can help them understand the juvenile. Using all of this information, the juvenile-court judge will come up with a sentence that is a plan for teaching the juvenile how not to be delinquent. Juveniles can be sentenced to anything from a warning to years in a detention center. However, their sentences can't go past the age of twenty-one and they cannot be sent to adult prison. Juvenile delinquents will be closely supervised by their probation officers, who will help them get whatever services a judge ordered. Juvenile delinquents will come back to court every year to check in with the judge, who will look at their progress and see if any adjustments need to be made to the sentence.

While criminal-court judges also possess discretion, their discretion can be limited by factors such as mandatory sentencing laws. These are laws requiring a judge to impose at least the minimum, but no more than the maximum, sentence contained in the law making whatever the person did a crime. Other mandatory sentencing laws prohibit judges from sentencing those

Judges are usually attorneys who have many years of experience practicing law before becoming judges. They are expected to rely on this knowledge and experience in sentencing.

found guilty to probation and require a term of imprisonment.

For example, federal drug laws say that someone convicted of having 3.5 ounces (100 grams) of heroin with the intention of selling it can't get fewer than five or more than forty years in prison. A judge would have to sentence a juvenile offender convicted of this crime to something between five and forty years. Criminal-court judges do have some discretion in that they can pick anything in that range.

However, they are still required to sentence juvenile offenders based on (1) what law was broken, (2) what punishment that law orders, and (3) how many other crimes the juvenile has committed.

There are some exceptions to mandatory sentencing laws that apply to juvenile offenders. The exceptions come from the Eighth Amendment's rule against "cruel and unusual punishment." The Supreme Court has said that it is cruel and unusual to give juveniles the death penalty because juveniles aren't as culpable as adults. Death is the ultimate punishment because it takes life and liberty. It is saved for people who commit the worst crimes and is meant to keep violent people who can't change off the streets. Because juveniles are still changing, they can't be punished with death.

Juvenile offenders can't automatically be given life without parole for murder. Nor can they be given that sentence for crimes other than murder. Parole is permission for a prisoner to leave prison before his or her full sentence is up. Good behavior can earn an inmate parole. Juvenile offenders can get life without parole, but only for murder and only after there has

The mandatory sentence for killing a federal officer is death or life in prison. A minor tried as an adult cannot receive the death penalty but can be sentenced to spend the rest of his life in federal prison.

been a hearing that focuses on the juvenile's ability to change. Juveniles can get life in prison for crimes other than murder, but they must have the chance for parole.

JUDICIAL DISCRETION: GOOD OR BAD?

More judicial discretion means how the case goes will depend on the judge. This can be good or bad for juveniles. A judge who thinks a case is weak or that what the juvenile did is no big deal might let them go. A judge who likes, believes, or feels sorry for a juvenile can order treatment instead of detention. A judge's discretion is more limited in most criminal cases. Comparatively speaking, a juvenile-court judge has more power to "go easy."

However, there being no rules means that juveniles are more vulnerable to a judge's personal biases. Juveniles of color are sent to pretrial detention more than white juveniles are. Male juveniles are more likely to have their case transferred to criminal court than are females. A juvenile-court judge who hates drugs might transfer every drug case to criminal court, while a judge who thinks it's normal for young people to experiment might keep the same cases in juvenile court. Judicial discretion makes it hard for juveniles to know what to expect in juvenile court. The sentencing guidelines for federal and state courts aren't entirely specific either, but they do give defendants some idea of what might be coming.

Some states have blended sentencing laws. These allow criminal-court judges to give juvenile offenders a sentence that is part juvenile, part criminal. The criminal part is put on hold, or "suspended," until after the juvenile serves the juvenile part of the sentence. A juvenile who doesn't get in trouble with the law again won't have to serve the adult portion of the sentence. If the juvenile is rearrested or violates the terms of his or her release, that juvenile will have to serve the rest of his or her sentence in an adult prison.

Whether or not a juvenile offender ends up in prison what will have the biggest effect on a juvenile's life. Adult prisons are for criminals, people who need to be punished or are too dangerous to be free. Prisons have harsh living conditions and are often violent. Juveniles are more likely to be victims of this violence. Juveniles have the hardest time recovering from such trauma because they are young and easy to influence. This also makes it easier for juvenile offenders to learn from adult inmates to be violent.

Prisons are harsh and violent places. Minors are impressionable, so being in prison increases the chances that a juvenile will be violent when released and be sent back to prison.

Most prisons don't have alcohol and drug treatment programs that are aimed specifically at juveniles, nor do they offer sex offender treatment, family counseling, and many other services that a juvenile delinquent would get. Without treatment and support, juvenile offenders are less likely to learn the life skills they will need when they are released. Juvenile offenders are more likely to commit crimes in the future, and their crimes will be more violent. Being treated as an adult increases the likelihood that a juvenile offender will come back through the criminal-justice system one or more times throughout his adulthood.

POSTRELEASE ISSUES

Juvenile offenders will also face more challenges when they are done with their sentences. They might be separated from other students if they go back to school, or they may be too old for school because of the length of their sentences. Juvenile offenders are less likely to get their high-school diplomas, making it harder for them to find high-paying jobs. They might have a hard time finding any job, since a lot of employers won't hire people with criminal records. Delinquency records, on the other hand, are usually confidential and won't show up on a background check.

In some states, juvenile offenders will never be able to vote even once they turn eighteen. This means that they will never get a say in what laws they have to follow. All of these factors combine to make it more likely that juvenile offenders will have less liberty in the long run.

CONCLUSION

The best way for people to protect their life and liberty is to know and use their constitutional rights. It is especially important for minors because they can be punished like adults, even though they are not as guilty. Adult punishments have large, negative impacts on juveniles, which is why they need to avoid the criminal-justice system. They must understand the law and the system if they want to do this. Knowledge is power. Juveniles with knowledge of their rights and the system can keep themselves and those they care about out of trouble. This will increase their chances of enjoying the life and liberty to which they are entitled under the Constitution.

GLOSSARY

action In law, another word for "case" or "proceeding."

arson Setting fire to another person's property.

assault Using or threatening to use force against another person.

attorney Another word for "lawyer."

circumstances The condition or facts that affect a situation.

conspiracy A group of two or more people who plan together to break the law.

corruption A public official lying about or hiding facts (called "fraud") or taking or keeping property he or she was put in charge of (called "embezzlement").

defendant A person who has been accused of a crime.

delinquent Someone who is guilty of doing something that would be a crime if done by an adult.

discretion In law, the power to decide what should happen when there is no law indicating what has to happen.

evidence Documents, items, testimony, statements, or anything else that can be used to establish a fact.

incriminate To say or do something that makes a person look guilty of a crime.

indictment An official piece of paper accusing someone of committing a crime.

jurisdiction Having the power to make judgments concerning a legal case.

juvenile defendant A minor accused of doing something that would be a crime if done by an adult.

minor A person under the age of eighteen.

petition A piece of paper accusing a juvenile of doing something that would be a crime if done by an adult.

presumption The belief that something is true, though it has yet to be proven.

prosecutor The lawyer for the state in a criminal or juvenile case.

vandalism Causing damage to someone else's property.

waiver The decision to give up a right. Judges can waive their court's jurisdiction over a case.

witness Someone who sees, hears, or otherwise knows about a crime.

FOR MORE INFORMATION

Campaign for Youth Justice
1220 L Street NW
Suite 605
Washington, DC 20005
(202) 558-3580
A not-for-profit organization dedicated to ending the practice of treating juveniles as adults in the adult criminal-justice system.

Canadian Children's Rights Council
5175 Yonge Street, Suite 105
Toronto, ON M2N 5P5
Canada
Toronto: (647) 933-2122
Ottawa: (613) 800-6474
A not-for-profit, nongovernmental organization focused on Canadian children's human rights.

Center for Children's Law and Policy
1701 K Street NW
Suite 1100
Washington, DC 20006
(202) 637-0377
A public interest law and policy organization focused on protecting the rights of children in the juvenile-and criminal-justice systems, currently working to reduce youth incarceration, reduce racial disparities in the juvenile-justice system, and improve conditions for confined youth.

Child Welfare League of America
1726 M Street NW

Suite 500
Washington, DC 20036
(202) 688-4200
A coalition of public and private agencies that works together to get better outcomes for vulnerable children and families.

Equal Justice Initiative
122 Commerce Street
Montgomery, Alabama 36104
(334) 269-1803
This not-for-profit organization provides legal representation to indigent defendants and prisoners, including juvenile offenders.

Justice for Children and Youth
Canadian Foundation for Children, Youth and the Law
415 Yonge Street, Suite 1203
Toronto, ON M5B 2E7
Canada
Local: (416) 920-1633
Ontario Toll-Free: 1-866-999-5329
A Canadian not-for-profit legal-aid organization focused on assisting and empowering children and youth, JFCY provides legal representation to low-income youth in and around Toronto, Ontario.

National Center for Youth Law
405 14th Street, 15th Floor
Oakland, CA 94612
(510) 835-8098
A not-for-profit organization focused on using the law to

protect low-income children, the NCYL "works to ensure that youth in trouble with the law are treated appropriately for their age and capacity to change."

Office of Juvenile Justice and Delinquency Prevention (OJJDP)
810 Seventh Street NW
Washington, DC 20531
(202) 307-5911
Housed within the United States Department of Justice, the OJJDP researches juvenile delinquency throughout the United States, makes recommendations, and helps state and local governments improve juvenile-justice policies and practices.

WEBSITES

Because of the changing nature of Internet links, Rosen Publishing has developed an online list of websites related to the subject of this book. This site is updated regularly. Please use this link to access the list:

http://www.rosenlinks.com/KYR/Juve

FOR FURTHER READING

Bates, Kristin A., and Richelle S. Swan. *Juvenile Delinquency in a Diverse Society.* Thousand Oaks, CA: SAGE Publications, Inc., 2013.

Bergman, Paul, and Sara Berman-Barrett. *The Criminal Law Handbook: Know Your Rights, Survive the System.* Berkley, CA: Nolo, 2013.

Brezina, Corona. *Frequently Asked Questions About Juvenile Detention.* New York, NY: Rosen Publishing Group, 2011.

Buckner, Melton, Jr. *The Law* (Criminal Justice). New York, NY: Chelsea House Publishing, 2010.

Christ, James. *Mad: How to Deal with Your Anger and Get Respect*. Minneapolis, MN: Free Spirit Publishing, Inc., 2007.

Evans, Colin. *Trials and the Courts.* New York, NY: Chelsea House Publishing, 2010.

Jacobs, Thomas. *Teens Take It to Court: Young People Who Challenged the Law—and Changed Your Life.* Revised & Updated Edition. Minneapolis, MN: Free Spirit Publishing, Inc., 2006.

Jacobs, Thomas. *They Broke the Law—You Be the Judge: True Cases of Teen Crime.* Minneapolis, MN: Free Spirit Publishing, Inc., 2003.

Jacobs, Thomas. *What are My Rights?: Q&A About Teens and the Law.* 3rd ed. Minneapolis, MN: Free Spirit Publishing, Inc., 2011.

Kayer, George. *The Best 500 Nonprofit Organizations for Prisoners and Their Families.* 1st ed. CreateSpace Independent Publishing Platform, 2013.

Krygier, Leora. *Juvenile Court: A Judge's Guide for Young Adults and Their Parents.* Lanham, MD: Scarecrow Press, Inc., 2008.

Kuklin, Susan. *No Choirboy: Murder, Violence, and Teenagers on Death Row.* New York, NY: Square Fish, 2014.

Lankford, Susan Madden. *Born, Not Raised: Voices from Juvenile Hall.* San Diego, CA: Humane Exposures Publishing, LLC, 2012.

Martin, Buzzy. *Don't Shoot! I'm the Guitar Man.* New York, NY: Berkley Trade, 2010.

Nurse, Anne M. *Locked Up, Locked Out: Young Men in the Juvenile Justice System.* Nashville, TN: Vanderbilt University Press, 2010.

Palmer, Pat. *Teen Esteem: A Self-Direction Manual for Young Adults.* 3rd ed. Atascadero, CA: Impact Publishers, Inc., 2010.

Simmons, Danette. *Teen Reflections: My Life, My Journey, My Story.* CreateSpace Independent Publishing Platform, 2010.

Sobel, Syl. *The U.S. Constitution and You.* 2nd ed. Hauppauge, NY: Baron's Educational Services, Inc., 2012.

Swan, Bill. *Real Justice: Fourteen and Sentenced to Death: The Story of Steven Truscott.* Toronto, ON: Lorimer, 2012.

Vaughan, Jenny. *Juvenile Crime* (Inside Crime). Smart Apple Media, 2011.

BIBLIOGRAPHY

Atkins v. Virginia, 536 U.S. 304 (2002)

Brinegar v. United States, 338 U.S. 160 (1949)

Bulman, P., *Bulletin: Delays in Youth Justice.* U.S. Department of Justice, Office of Juvenile Justice and Delinquency Prevention, February 2014. Retrieved March 9, 2014 (https://ncjrs.gov/pdffiles1/nij/237149.pdf).

Delo v. Lashley, 507 U.S. 272 (1993)

Estelle v. Williams, 425 U.S. 501 (1976)

Graham v. Florida, 560 U.S. 48 (2010)

Griffin, P., P. Torbet, and L. Szymanski, *Trying Juveniles as Adults in Criminal Court: An Analysis of State Transfer Provisions.* Office of Juvenile Justice and Delinquency Prevention, December 1998. Retrieved March 12, 2014 (http://www.ojjdp.gov/pubs/tryingjuvasadult/toc.html)

Howell, J., B. Field, D. Mears, R. Loeber, and D. Petechuk. *Bulletin 5: Young Offenders and an Effective Response in the Juvenile and Adult Justice Systems: What Happens, What Should Happen, and What We Need to Know.* (Study Group on the Transitions Between Juvenile Delinquency and Adult Crime). U.S. Department of Justice, July 2013. Retrieved March 12, 2014 (https://ncjrs.gov/pdffiles1/nij/grants/242935.pdf)

In re Gault, 387 U.S. 1 (1967)

In re Winship, 397 U.S. 358 (1970)

Kent v. United States, 383 U.S. 541 (1964)

Lazarow, Katherine. *The Continued Viability of New York's Juvenile Offender Act in Light of Recent National Developments.* 57 N.Y.L. Sch. L. Rev. 595 (2012/2013)

Massachusetts General Laws ch. 265, et seq.
Massachusetts General Laws, ch. 266, et seq.
Massachusetts General Laws, ch. 267A, et seq.
Massachusetts General Laws, ch. 272, et seq.
McKeiver v. Pennsylvania, 403 U.S. 528 (1971)
Miller v. Alabama, 132 S. Ct. 2455 (June 25, 2012)
Miranda v. Arizona, 384 U.S. 436 (1966)
Moore v. United States, 160 U.S. 268 (1895)
Neder v. United States, 527 U.S. 1 (1999)
Office of General Counsel, U.S. Sentencing Commission, *Drug Primer.* March 2013. Retrieved March 9, 2014 (http://www.ussc.gov/Legal/Primers/Primer_Drug.pdf)
Puzzanchera, C. and S. Hockenberry, *Juvenile Court Statistics 2010. National Center for Juvenile Justice and Office of Juvenile Justice and Delinquency Prevention*, June 2013. Retrieved March 2, 2014 (http://www.ojjdp.gov/ojstatbb/njcda/pdf/jcs2010.pdf).
Roper v. Simmons, 543 U.S. 551 (2005)
Rubin, T., "The Future of Children; the Juvenile Court," *The Nature of the Court Today*, Princeton University and the Brookings Institution, Vol. 6, No. 3 (Winter 1996). Retrieved January 23, 2014 (http://futureofchildren.org/futureofchildren/publications/journals/journal_details/index.xml?journalid=55)
Steinberg, Laurence, "The Future of Children; Juvenile Justice," *Introducing the Issue.* Princeton University and the Brookings Institution, Vol. 18, No. 2 (Fall 2008). Retrieved January 23, 2014 (http://futureofchildren.org/futureofchildren/publications/journals/journal_details/index.xml?journalid=31)

Stevenson, C., C. Larson, L. Carter, D. Gomby, D. Terman, and R. Behrman, "The Future of Children; the Juvenile Court," *The Juvenile Court: Analysis and Recommendations.* Princeton University and the Brookings Institution, Vol. 6, No. 3 (Winter 1996). Retrieved January 23, 2014 (http://futureofchildren.org/futureofchildren/publications/journals/journal_details/index.xml?journalid=55)

United States v. Wong, 40 F.3d 1347 (2d Cir. 1994)

INDEX

ABOUT THE AUTHOR

Cristen Nagle is an attorney in Rochester, New York. She has clerked for the justices of the Massachusetts Superior Court and an associate justice of the Massachusetts Appeals Court. As a solo practitioner, Nagle handles all types of cases, including family law. She is a graduate of the University at Buffalo Law School and Mount Holyoke College.

ABOUT THE EXPERT REVIEWER

Lindsay A. Lewis, Esq., is a practicing criminal defense attorney in New York City, where she handles a wide range of matters, from those discussed in this series to high-profile federal criminal cases. She believes that each and every defendant deserves a vigorous and informed defense. Lewis is a graduate of the Benjamin N. Cardozo School of Law and Vassar College.

PHOTO CREDITS

Cover Shane Hansen/E+/Getty Images; cover background Christophe Rolland/Shutterstock.com; pp. 4–5 Image Source/Photodisc/Getty Images; p. 8 The Washington Post/Getty Images; p. 11 Richard Legg/E+/Getty Images; pp. 12–13 Fuse/Thinkstock; p. 14 BigRedCurlyGuy/iStock/Thinkstock; pp. 16–17 Hill Street Studios/Matthew Palmer/Blend Images/Getty Images; pp. 20–21, 45 moodboard/Thinkstock; p. 24 Trista Weibell/E+/Getty Images; p. 26 sam74100/iStock/Thinkstock; pp. 28–29 Steve Debenport/E+/Getty Images; p. 31 © AP Images; p. 33 Amos Morgan/Photodisc/Thinkstock; p. 35 Mona Makela/Shutterstock.com; pp. 36–37 Fuse/Thinkstock; p. 40 Image Source/Getty Images; p. 42 Chris Ryan/OJO Images/Getty Images; pp. 46–47 justasc/Shutterstock.com; p. 49 Jupiterimages/Stockbyte/Getty Images.

Designer: Brian Garvey; Editor: Jeanne Nagle